John Cooper was born in Paris, Illinois, on January 15, 1949. He was baptised Roman Catholic and grew up on his father's and uncles' farms. After graduating from Marshall, IL High School, he attended Samford University in Birmingham, AL. He left college and became a cabinetmaker, having his own business for about 45 years. About three years ago, he returned to the Catholic Church of his youth. Having recently passed along his business to a younger person, John attended Spring Hill College in Mobile, AL, finishing his requirements for a Certificate in Spiritual Direction (CSD) in the Summer of 2019.

To my wife, Wynema (Wink) Cooper, who has patiently
supported me during the writing of this book.

John Cooper

LET GOD IN: ONE IGNATIAN JOURNEY

AUSTIN MACAULEY PUBLISHERS™

LONDON · CAMBRIDGE · NEW YORK · SHARJAH

A CIP catalogue record for this title is available from the British Library.

ISBN 9781528927482 (Paperback)
ISBN 9781528927499 (Hardback)
ISBN 9781528965095 (ePub e-book)

www.austinmacauley.com

First Published (2019)
Austin Macauley Publishers Ltd
25 Canada Square
Canary Wharf
London
E14 5LQ

Thanks to Sr. Madeleine Gregg, fcJ
(My 19th Annotation Spiritual Director)
Thanks to Wynema (Wink) Cooper
(My wife of over forty years)
Thanks to Vikram Bhatia
(My first pass editor)
Thanks to Margaret (Meghan) Johnston
(My second pass editor)
Thanks to Fran and Kathie Viselli,
Genevieve Snipes, and Judith Sculley
(Who experienced the 19th Annotation alongside me)
Thanks to Andrew Yankech
(My Substantive Editor)
Spring Hill College, Mobile, AL
(Where I study for a Certificate in Spiritual Direction)

Table of Contents

Introduction

Let me tell you my story. I am a cabinetmaker who has been in the cabinet industry for over forty years. However, I have learned as a result of this Ignatian journey that my core identity is actually that of a sinner, but a sinner loved by God. I have learned a new non-dual identity that I am already blessed and was placed before my birth into an eternal unity with the Divine One, as are all of us since we are all created in God's image. This is who I am and this may be who you discover you are also.

I was led to Ignatian spirituality while experiencing major business downturns during the Great Recession beginning in 2007. Those downturns eventually lead to bankruptcy. I thought I was in pretty good shape, having saved up quite a bit of money and diversified my business to include imports as well. I actually did well the first year of the recession, but as the banking industry became increasingly unstable and available credit closed up, and due to some unwise financial decisions on my part, my personal and business situation worsened dramatically. In addition, my customers were going out of business and/or cutting back on costs to such an extent that I couldn't afford to take on some jobs at the prices they were willing to pay. I lost my three-person sales crew.

In the midst of all this, I looked up 'decision making' on the internet. It was there I discovered the principles of Ignatian discernment. I found some information here, more information there, but nothing comprehensive. Eventually, I discussed what I was investigating with Sr. Madeleine Gregg, fcJ, a spiritual director in the Ignatian tradition. This link will lead to where Sr. Madeleine now practices Spiritual Direction: https://www.fcjcentre.ca/resourceteam. She gladly agreed to help. I was to be her first directee. We ended up also asking four others to join in a small group to begin the 19th Annotation Spiritual Retreat. This is how I came to begin my personal discovery of Ignatian spirituality.

What did this journey mean to me? In my case, I was a 'cradle' Catholic and a lifelong Christian, baptised and confirmed in the Catholic Church. Around twenty years of age, I had an adult conversion experience as a part of my desire to follow Jesus' teachings, and I became a conscientious objector to war.

I have been baptised, confirmed, baptised again, ordained a deacon, ordained an elder, and commissioned as a pastor. I served as a bi-vocational pastor for seven years. I have been blessed to serve in many leadership capacities, but this journey into Ignatian spirituality has been another life-changing occurrence. Ignatian spirituality has been for me another opportunity to repent, to be formed again, to be converted again, and to enter a higher state of purification which, hopefully, will never end.

Before one begins an Ignatian spiritual retreat, it is important to begin with the right dispositions. Why are we here? What are we supposed to do in this life? What is the end goal of our lives? St. Ignatius terms this the *First Principle and Foundation*. Here is a translation of what St. Ignatius said regarding this *First Principle and Foundation* drawn from *The Spiritual Exercises of St. Ignatius:*[1]

---

[1] *The Spiritual Exercises of St. Ignatius, a New Translation based on Studies in the Language of the Autograph*, by Ludovico J. Puhl, S.J., Loyola Press, 1951, ISBN: 10: 0-8294-0065-6.

Man is created to praise, reverence, and serve God our Lord, and by this means to save his soul.
The other things on the face of the Earth are created for man to help him in attaining the end for which he is created.
Hence man is to make use of them in as far as they help him in the attainment of his end, and he must rid himself of them in as far as they prove a hindrance to him.
Therefore, we must make ourselves indifferent to all created things, as far as we are allowed free choice and are not under any prohibition. Consequently, as far as we are concerned, we should not prefer health to sickness, riches to poverty, honour to dishonour, a long life to a short life. The same holds for all other things.[2]

As we fall into the arms of God, our Lord, beginning here, on this earth, we realise St. Ignatius must be referring to more than just some kind of 'beatific vision' in which we gaze upon the beauty of God, our Lord for all eternity. The understanding that we are created in love and to love, reverence, and praise God morphs itself into 'affectionate awe' which we express throughout this life on earth now and in eternity. Our praise, our worship, is more than playing harps and singing songs to our Lord, God. This worship and praise is actually learning to know Him more clearly, to follow Him more nearly, and to love Him more dearly. As to saving our souls, which we cannot do of our own power, we find that Jesus' death and resurrection accomplishes the task of saving our souls, but we can willingly participate in the salvation process by dying to our own desires and our own life, our own attachments and addictions, resting in His provision for us and trusting in His grace for the

---

[2] Ibid, p. 12

resurrection of our souls and bodies. It is possible to read the *First Principle and Foundation* thinking St. Ignatius recommends we obtain our own salvation, but this is not what he actually means. The First Principle and Foundation show us God's purpose for mankind, which includes growing in love of Christ and authentic discipleship.

I know a man in his 90s who has lived a good life. He fought in WWII on the Beach of Normandy. He told me bodies of his fellow soldiers were falling all around him but he was not killed. "Wow!" I said, "You must have a purpose in your life!" Ignatius tells us we all have a purpose right at the start of *The First Principle and Foundation*. Ignatius states: "Man is created to praise, reverence, and serve God, our Lord, and by this means to save his soul" (SpEx, p. 12).

When I read the First Principle and Foundation, I thought it meant that this would be a work of our own doing—to save our own souls by praising, reverencing, and serving our Lord. But of course, salvation is not earned; it is granted.

Considering the significance of the *Principle and Foundation* to Ignatian spiritual seekers today, I believe it is essential to properly understand the importance of Grace to the *Spiritual Exercises* and specifically to the *First Principle and Foundation*. We will see that St. Ignatius understood grace in relationship to salvation from the perspective of Catholic thinking in his time. He had attended the University of Paris, the best university in Europe and understood the nature of Catholic theology from a both/and, not either/or point of view. Ignatian Spirituality and this unitive type of spirituality calls us to divine union with the one mysterious God. We are saved and created for good works which includes praising, reverencing, and serving God, our Lord, as Ignatius mentions.

We see St. Ignatius growing in grace and knowledge throughout the *Spiritual Exercises*. Grace or a form of grace is mentioned about forty times in the *Exercises*. When I read the First Principle and Foundation, I thought it meant that this would be a work of our own doing—to save our own souls by praising, reverencing, and serving our Lord. But of course, salvation is not earned; it is granted. *Rules for Thinking with the Church*, Ignatius states:

Granted that it be very true that no one can be saved without being predestined and without having faith and grace, still we must be cautious about the way in which we speak of all these things and discuss them with others (SpEx p. 160).

The caution Ignatius urges is in view of Martin Luther's reformation and the beliefs concerning predestination in his age, but Ignatius admits to the impossibility of salvation without grace but asked those in his care to be careful in discussing the matter. He speaks of grace in rule 369, 17, arguing for free will, not predestination:

Likewise, we ought not to speak of grace at such length and with such emphasis that the poison of doing away with liberty in engendered (SpEx p. 161).

Throughout the *Exercises,* the concept of God's grace is promoted. The primacy of grace in Catholic thought and doctrine is now and was in Ignatius' time well understood. Ignatius' unitive thinking meant that grace actually works when given by God to humans. It is crucial to read the *First Principle and Foundation* in view of grace. One just cannot save himself. Therefore, Ignatius gradually weaves in the doctrine of grace throughout the *Exercises,* here a little, and there a little.

For instance, let us look at *Rules for the Discernment of Spirits* 320, 7:

He can resist with the help of God, which always remains, though he may not clearly perceive it. For though God has taken from him the abundance of fervour and overflowing love and the intensity of His favours, nevertheless, He has sufficient grace for eternal salvation (SpEx p. 143).

Grace is foundational in St. Ignatius' eyes for salvation. Ignatius and the Jesuits were instrumental in the Catholic Counter Reformation and the Council of Trent. Because God first calls us, and allows us to freely choose our response to His initial Grace, one might think of first *Principle and Foundation* in this way:

[By Grace] Man is created to praise, reverence, and serve God our Lord, [by grace,] and by this means [grace] to save his soul [by grace, through faith, the work of God.]

Our response to God's saving work in us and our thankfulness for God's first calling us is a desire to do more for God, thus works are responses to grace in every case. It is crucial for those who give the *Spiritual Exercises* to others to understand the grace-filled meaning of the *First Principle and Foundation* right from the start and let everybody know right from the beginning that we are all loved sinners saved by God's grace to do good works. Grace works!

Some of the questions Sr. Madeleine asked us to consider before beginning the retreat included: What is preventing me from praising and serving God? Do I believe God's creation is a gift to me? What is preventing me from seeing God's love? And what is it

18

that keeps me from experiencing God's comforting embrace?

The Ignatian retreat is focused upon prayer in general and upon the Holy Spirit in particular as it moves within each individual to bring and renew spiritual maturity. If one has already been born again, one can experience even another transformation as the Holy Spirit teaches us. It is not the job of the retreat leader to 'teach' the retreat, as I understand it, but it is to serve as a faithful companion, observing how the Holy Spirit teaches and works in the retreatant's life.

This is just my story, and maybe one day you will be sharing your story with me. This is a way to love one another—to listen to each other's stories.

Who Was St. Ignatius of Loyola?

I have referred to Ignatian spirituality and an Ignatian retreat, so by now you are probably wondering, 'What are these things?' It all began with a young Spaniard, Ignatius of Loyola, born in 1491. Early in his life, he planned to pursue the typical goals of a young nobleman: adventure, glory, and royal favour. While recovering from a serious injury in battle, he experienced a deep conversion and decided to dedicate his life to Christ. As part of his conversion, he gave up his sword and laid it in front of a statue of Mary at the Benedictine Monastery in Montserrat, Spain, and entered a more peaceful and nonviolent way of life. He eventually wrote *The Spiritual Exercises*, founded the Society of Jesus (also known as the Jesuits), and moved to Rome. The spirituality he experienced became a way of life and continual conversion. Ignatius learned to leave his sins in the past and to press forward into deeper and deeper spirituality. Ignatius' seeking resulted in a pilgrimage to Montserrat, to Jerusalem, to Rome, to Spain, to France, and back to Rome, and various places, but really, his crucial journey was an inner journey to the Kingdom of God, which was within himself.

His journey and spirituality were so radical for its time that Ignatius was called before the inquisition for examination concerning his 'way of life', but nothing wrong could be found, and he was ordered not to speak of his faith or the things of God. Ignatius could not quit speaking of God.

The Holy Spirit led him onwards in his journey. Even time in prison could not stop Ignatius. The 'desires' Ignatius had for God would not go away. The problem the institutional Church had with him was that Ignatius was not 'learned'. Therefore, Ignatius went to school at an older age than his fellow students. Eventually, he finished school and was ordained a priest and found favour with the Pope before creating the Society of Jesus. Within only a few decades, the Jesuits had founded universities all around Europe and Jesuit missionaries spread all over the world. The Jesuits are the largest order of priests in the Catholic Church and are dedicated to the causes of higher education, social justice, and solidarity with the poor and marginalised. *The Spiritual Exercises* provide a way of encountering and developing a relationship with God through Jesus Christ and have inspired countless people over nearly five hundred years.

What are the Spiritual Exercises?

As if one were to do physical exercises, adding new and different ones as one develops, or repeating the same ones over and over until one grows in strength, so it is like this in some ways with the Spiritual Exercises. I quote Louis J. Puhl, SJ, who translated a popular version of the Exercises, below:

I. "By the term 'Spiritual Exercises' is meant every method of examination of conscience, of meditation, of contemplation, of vocal and mental prayer, and of other spiritual activities that will be mentioned later. For just as taking a walk, journeying on foot, and running are bodily exercises, so we call Spiritual Exercises every way of preparing and disposing the soul to rid itself of all inordinate attachments, and, after their removal, of seeking and finding the will of God in the disposition of our life for the salvation of our soul.

II. (002)

"The one who explains to another the method and order of meditating or contemplating should narrate accurately the facts of the contemplation or meditation. Let him adhere to the points, and add only a short or summary explanation. The reason for this is that when one in meditating takes the solid foundation of facts, and goes over it and reflects on it for himself, he may find something that makes them a little clearer or better understood. This may arise either from his own reasoning, or from the grace of God enlightening his mind. Now, this produces greater spiritual relish and fruit than if one in giving the Exercises had explained and developed the meaning at great length. For it is not much knowledge that fills and satisfies the soul, but the intimate understanding and relish of the truth.

III. (003)

"In all the Spiritual Exercises which follow, we make use of the acts of the intellect in reasoning, and of the acts of the will in manifesting our love. However, we must observe that when in acts of the will we address God our Lord or His saints either vocally or mentally, greater reverence is required on our part than when we use the intellect in reasoning."

The Spiritual Exercises begin with twenty preliminary notes, or annotations, about the Exercises. The overarching theme is one of *adaptability*—the Exercises are not a rigid prescription for how to encounter God. Rather, the goal is to draw oneself closer to God, and just as each person is unique, and each relationship we have is unique, so too the ways in each of us deepens our relationship with God will be unique.

The Exercises themselves are organised into four 'weeks' with several preparation days in the beginning. These are not weeks in the traditional sense of time, but phases or movements one experiences as he or she prays through the Exercises.

The 19th Annotation:

The 19th Annotation, sometimes referred to as a 'retreat in daily life', which is the method I took to experience the Exercises, is usually given to men and women who do not have the time or resources to take a full thirty-day retreat, which is how St. Ignatius originally envisioned the Exercises. Because he wanted the Exercises and their benefits to be available to everyone, Ignatius created an alternate manner of experiencing them spread out over an extended period of time. He describes this alternative in the 19th Annotation to the Exercises, thus the name for this form of retreat. I took the 19th Annotation in a small group setting, led by Sr. Madeleine Gregg, fcJ. Sometimes the 19th Annotation is also given individually. I know of a spiritual director who is giving the 19th Annotation to a directee with only occasional in person contact. The director and directee are using a video-conferencing service over the internet since they each live in different states. One must set aside about one hour each day for prayer, reflection, and journaling your thoughts after prayer. This time may be more effective early in the morning. In addition, another fifteen minutes or so is devoted to the Examen prayer in review of one's day before falling asleep.

The foundation of Christian spiritual direction is Christ's presence living in us. Human guides or companions listen with the directee for the calling of the Holy Spirit, who is the authentic spiritual guide. The Spirit is active in all spiritual exercises including our own daily life. Spiritual directors, or more accurately spiritual guides or companions, pray with and accompany directees as the Holy Spirit directly communicates the desires (a better term than 'will') of God for the directee.

Please permit me to share my journey with you along with the Scripture basis for my prayers and reflections and some helpful Ignatian-based quotes. It is not necessary to read this book all at once. These reflections follow my thoughts and emotions as I experienced the Exercises while going through serious financial hardship. If you are going through the 19th Annotation yourself, you may find it helpful to read a reflection each week. Or if you are considering making the Exercises, perhaps reading this book will convince you of the value of opening your heart to God in this manner. Regardless, I hope that you will find something in the pages that follow that reveals God's loving grace a little more clearly to you.

Author's Note

This book is a condensation of my personal journal as I took the 19th Annotation of the Spiritual Exercises of St. Ignatius. The form you are reading is a devotional, not meant to be read as quickly as possible, but to be read with your personal daily prayers and reflections. You may wish to spend a few minutes each day or week reading this book and praying with the Scriptures and quotations therein and write your own journal if the Holy Spirit guides you to do so. My purpose in sharing my journey through the 19th Annotation of the Spiritual Exercises of St. Ignatius is to encourage you, the reader, through the lens of Grace and Peace, to explore Ignatian prayer as one way to encounter the living Christ yourself and in yourself by reflecting on Him as you read this book. By integrating Scripture, reflective quotations, and my own personal story of financial hardship coupled with spiritual growth, I endeavour to share with you this nearly five hundred-year-old form of spirituality. Perhaps you may even be inspired to take an Ignatian retreat yourself. I hope that this book will promote Ignatian spirituality for both Catholics and non-Catholics, and even those of non-Christian beliefs. Please find a place and a time to pray and let God into your life!

There are various forms of prayer. The principle type of prayer upon which this book is based is *Lectio Divina*, or the reading of Scripture, the meditation on Scripture, and contemplations which may occur during these processes of prayer. These contemplations, given by God, without your effort, may turn into prayers of imagination, where you are placed in the scene of the

Scriptures on which you are meditating, or imagine yourself to be a companion of Jesus or another biblical figure. This form of prayer is not about 'asking' God for our needs, or necessarily the needs of others. The Ignatian method of prayer is about *listening* to God, *experiencing* God, *feeling* God's presence within us.

At the end of your day, I suggest you pray the Ignatian Examen which is a way of prayer to review your day, to consider where and how God has been present to you in all things, to review your shortcomings without judging yourself, but asking forgiveness as needed, to appreciate the Graces of the day God has given you, and to consider your goals for the next day. If you want to learn more about the Examen, I suggest visiting the website www.IgnatianSpirituality.com. There, you can find much information about Ignatian spirituality in general and the Examen in particular, including this five-step version of the daily Examen that St. Ignatius practiced:

1. Become aware of God's presence and give thanks.
2. Petition God, asking for the Graces you desire.
3. Review the day with gratitude, paying attention to your emotions.
4. Face your shortcomings and ask forgiveness.
5. Look toward tomorrow, setting a spiritual goal for the day.

Finally, as you read through the following pages, you will come across references to the Gospel of Peace. I believe that one of the many ways in which Ignatian spirituality leads us to Jesus Christ is through an implicit call to non-violence. After all, as mentioned above, St. Ignatius, himself once a vain and glory seeker soldier, gave up his weapons and laid them at the feet of a statue of Mary. Violence, aggression, intimidation—these are among the disordered attachments Ignatius encourages us to set aside as we seek to discover God's dream for our lives.

When I speak of the Gospel of Peace, I speak of the teachings of Jesus expressed in the Sermon on the Mount when He taught the vision for the Kingdom of God for His new government, active in our hearts and souls with instructions we are to actually follow when we follow Him, such as expressed in His desire that we should love our enemies, do good to those who despitefully use us, and give up our attachments to this world's systems, and to love each other as He loved us. Before we begin, please allow me to share my personal prayer of formation I composed at the beginning of the *Exercises* and modified as needed as I took the *Exercises*.

Prayer of Formation/Disposition

Holy, Holy, Holy, Lord God Almighty,
El, Eli, Allah, Abba, Father, Jesus, Holy Spirit,
Isa, Great I AM,
Worthy is your name,
Worthy are all your names,
One Triune God, one in substance,
Help me to freely and continually
Give back
My life to you,
All of it,
And to live only
In your
Love and Grace, and to rest in you,
Aware of your presence in me,
Giving up my conceit, pride,
Deceit, vanity, arrogance,
Self-righteousness,
Disordinate affections,

And other sins,
Knowing every sin
Will not disappear
Until you raise me again
To eternal life,
Knowing that you love me,
Unconditionally,
Without limits,
And that I love you too,
Listening for your footsteps
As you walk with me,
And awaiting…
With eagerness and expectations
Of the gifts I hope to
Continuously receive from you,
Holy Spirit.
Father, I anticipate
Some of my future failings and sins,
But your Love, Grace, and Mercy
Are enough for me.
Jesus, I thank you
For all you have done
And are doing,
Not just for me,
But for all mankind,
Friends and enemies,
Having made peace with us,
On the cross.
Let me now be an instrument of
That same peace, and
The Mystery of the Gospel,
And the Mystery of the Kingdom,
To always be a vessel of your love, oh God,
And to glorify your name, Yahweh,
Forever
And ever,
Forever,
Amen.

Here are some other things you may want to consider before you pray.

Preparation for Prayer: Where will one pray? What posture? What material? How Long?

During Prayer: Have you created a space where you are prepared to not just talk *to* God, but also to talk *with* God? (This is especially important if you are relatively new to prayer.) Will you read, sing, think, listen? Are you open to responding to the feelings the Holy Spirit will stir within you?

After Prayer: Have a journal by your side to describe and reflect on your prayer session. Focus less on the specific things you prayed about and more on the feelings and emotions they elicited within you. The consolations (emotions that draw one closer to God) and the desolations (emotions of feeling distanced from God) are how God speaks to us.

Below is a picture of my particular place of prayer. Of course, your place does not need to be exactly like this, and you may not even be able to designate a physical space only for your prayer. The point is to create a physical sanctuary, even if only temporarily, so that you can experience an interior sanctuary. I like to have candles burning, and the ceramic cross on the wall was a gift from a dear friend. On the cross are the words, "Lord, make me an instrument of your peace." On the arm of the chair is a lap blanket I use in the cold winter mornings when I rise before daylight to pray.

Prayer is like exercising. You can't expect to jump in and be able to bench press 200 pounds right away. But with time, practice, and perseverance, you can work up to that. Start with small steps—a quiet place where you feel calm, pray for a short period of time—and pay attention to how you feel. Before long, when we take time out to be aware of God's presence and love, we'll come to realise that we want more of it and we are able to practice it longer and more deeply. Start with reasonable expectations of yourself, and you'll quickly be amazed at the results you'll feel inside.

Week One

But now thus says the Lord: Do not fear, for I have redeemed you; I have called you by name, you are mine. When you pass through the waters, I will be with you; and through the rivers, they shall not overwhelm you; when you walk through fire you shall not be burned, and the flame shall not consume you.
Isaiah 43:1–2

I do not believe that this passage promises that I will experience no pain or loss of material goods, but as we give up all but what God wants us to retain for His glory, we are brought through disasters with refined wills to return to God and return the love and grace He gives us. I began this retreat as a circuitous response to asking for advice about what I should do next in life as a result of potential financial failures. I am doing what is called the 19th Annotation, which is for those who must work and cannot go on a thirty-day retreat. As if a sign that life continues to go on even as we attempt to discern the right path forward, a walk-in prospect for the commercial property I need to sell dropped by.

Today begins the actual first 'week'[3] of four 'weeks' of the Ignatian Spirituality Retreat. The

---

[3] It has taken a long 'time' to get to the beginning of the first 'week'. In Ignatian Spirituality, time is not of the essence, and the meanings of time in our lives are altered. A 'week' is not necessarily a week, but a period of reflection. One may be

goal, or 'grace we desire', is to come to the awareness of sin, injustice, and evil in the world and continually celebrate Jesus' victory over the sin, injustice, and evil in the world. In other words, we celebrate the victory of living in the Kingdom of God. We seem to have an inner knowledge of sin, as if we are born into it. Some Theologians attribute this problem to the sin of Adam and Eve, but we open our eyes daily to see sin all around us, violence and war, greed, and even our own inaction or sins of omission whereby we know to do good, and do not do it. Yet, we know God loves us, despite our sin. God is merciful. We are loved.

Tomorrow, I eagerly await what God has for me and resolve to hear and answer when He calls.

The Grace We Seek: to be more aware of God's presence and personal love for me.

I call consolation every increase of faith, hope, and love, and all interior joy that invites and attracts to what is heavenly and to the salvation of one's soul by filling it with peace and quiet in its Creator and Lord.

Ignatius of Loyola,
The Spiritual Exercises of St. Ignatius

Week Two

I consider that the sufferings of this time are not worth comparing with the glory about to be revealed to us. We know that the whole creation has been groaning in labour pains until now; and not only the creation, but we ourselves, who have the first fruits of the Spirit, groan inwardly while we wait for adoption, the redemption of our bodies.

Romans 8:18, 22–23

I again realised the presence of God when my realtor brought in another prospect for my property besides the one I worked with on my own yesterday. I realise all is in God's hands and that God owns the whole world and all that is in it. I have already given up the property in my mind if it is God's will. I would not want to have to make the monthly payments into bankruptcy court, but I give up my will to live only to the mercy and grace of God's will.

The Grace We Seek: gratitude for the gift of creation.

Where is our God in suffering? We Christians do not have a fully satisfying explanation for why the world contains so much suffering. But we have something better: We have the power to deal with the suffering. We know where our God is during suffering. Our God is with us.

Richard Hauser, SJ, Finding God in Troubled Times

Week Three

I pray that, according to the riches of his glory, he may grant that you may be strengthened in your inner being with power through his Spirit, and that Christ may dwell in your hearts through faith, as you are being rooted and grounded in love. I pray that you may have the power to comprehend, with all the saints, what is the breadth and length and height and depth, and to know the love of Christ that surpasses knowledge, so that you may be filled with all the fullness of God.
Ephesians 3:16–19

Yesterday, it came up about one of my salespeople taking contracts and customers, getting set up with two of our cabinet vendors, and leaving us. I need to freely accept God's grace of forgiveness and completely forgive him and thank him for helping to bring my financial difficulties to a head. I may have to declare bankruptcy, which is a forgiveness of debts in itself. If I am forgiven of my sins by grace, through faith, I need to in grace, forgive all others.

The Grace We Seek: a deepening trust in God.

When we pray, we move inward to our God centre. Then we move out again...to our situation in the world. This movement into the centre and out again brings about an act of transformation... Usually there is a subtle, gentle, almost indiscernible change in our way of being that will carry its healing, changing power out through the layers of our lived experience and infuse the Where of our lives with its Kingdom values. This happens every time we pray, whether we are aware of it or not.

Margaret Silf, Inner Compass

Week Four

Yet whatever gains I had, these I have come to regard as loss because of Christ. More than that, I regard everything as loss because of the surpassing value of knowing Christ Jesus my Lord. For his sake I have suffered the loss of all things, and I regard them as rubbish, in order that I may gain Christ and be found in him, not having a righteousness of my own that comes from the law, but one that comes through faith in Christ, the righteousness from God based on faith.

Philippians 3:7–9

One of the reasons I am doing these Ignatian Exercises is to seek divine intervention regarding a transition in my life. What should I do for the rest of my life? This should be a question for each of our upcoming days, and every day forward. For me, career direction is needed. It is a perfect opportunity to let go of what once worked and once was within God's will to seek what God wants me to do now. Jesus said, "Truly, truly, I say to you, the Son can do nothing of his own accord." I think it is when I try to reason everything out while depending upon my own abilities, that failure occurs.

The Grace We Seek: awareness of attachments that prevent me from connecting with God, others, or myself.

It is not only prayer that gives God glory but work. Smiting on an anvil, sawing a beam, whitewashing a wall, driving horses, sweeping, scouring, everything gives God some glory if being in his grace you do it as your duty… He is so great that all things give him glory if you mean they should.

Gerard Manley Hopkins, SJ, Poems and Prose

Week Five

In the beginning was the Word, and the Word was with God, and the Word was God. He was in the beginning with God. All things came into being through him, and without him, not one thing came into being. What has come into being in him was life, and the life was the light of all people. The light shines in the darkness, and the darkness did not overcome it.

John 1:1–5

While reading the first chapter of the Gospel of John, I was reminded that God (the Word, Jesus that is) made all things and that without Him, nothing was made. I was reminded of the Spirit God breathed into man which makes mankind a living soul, different from animals, with God's own image stamped in us; this image, Quakers call a 'spark of God', in every person. Our self-transcendence seems to essentially be the recognition and feeling of this inner presence of God in not just us, but in everything and especially in every person.

The Grace We Seek: accepting my calling to praise, love, and serve God and others.

How much do you value the water that comes from your tap? We treat our relationships rather like that. They are just there… But relationship is a gift greater than today's sun, and each person give to you to love and be loved by is as indispensable as the pure water you thoughtlessly drink.

Joseph A. Tetlow, SJ, Examen: Persons in Relationship

Week Six

Above all, maintain constant love for one another, for love covers a multitude of sins. Be hospitable to one another without complaining. Like good stewards of the manifold grace of God, serve one another with whatever gift each of you has received.

1 Peter 4:8–10

In reflecting on 1 Peter 4:8–11, I came to realise that this gift of grace, the light which God gives us individually in varied ways as fruits of the Spirit, is a matter of self-transcendence. This transcendence reveals to us that the gifts we all have from the Holy Spirit are communal gifts, given to each of us in a variety of ways to be shared with all. It is in this way we become Evangelists to those who live in unbelief and share the Gospel in the world, sharing the light we have been given for the glory of God.

The Grace We Seek: awareness of the many ways God calls us.

Eternal Lord of all things, in the presence of Thy infinite goodness, and of Thy glorious mother, and of all the saints of Thy heavenly court, this is the offering of myself which I make with Thy favour and help. I protest that it is my earnest desire and my deliberate choice, provided only it is for Thy greater service and praise, to imitate Thee in bearing all wrongs and all abuse and all poverty, both actual and spiritual, should Thy most holy majesty deign to choose and admit me to such a state and way of life.

Ignatius of Loyola,
The Spiritual Exercises of St. Ignatius

39

The First Week
Week Seven

For while we were still weak, at the right time Christ died for the ungodly. Indeed, rarely will anyone die for a righteous person—though perhaps for a good person someone might actually dare to die. But God proves his love for us in that while we still were sinners, Christ died for us. Much more surely then, now that we have been justified by his blood, will we be saved through him from the wrath of God.

Romans 5:6–9

Questions about where I am at in my life and the way forward are what have led me to this exploration of Ignatian spirituality. Sometimes, I am reminded of the two cats my wife, Wink, and I keep in our basement. These cats recognise the steps of both of us and run to meet us when we walk down the stairs. When our cats hear the steps of a stranger, even if we are with the stranger, they run and hide. We should know the steps of God in our lives. I should know and seek those steps in my life, freely admitting my sins because I know God still loves me, and run to Him, as the cats run to Wink and me. The steps of the enemy, Satan, should be the ones from which I flee. The Holy Spirit is always welcome in my life and is ever with me, and I continually seek to be filled by the Holy Spirit.

Let me share a prayer I wrote the day before Pentecost, 2016, which I received in meditation:

Holy Spirit,
Worthy is your name,
Holy is your name,
If we knew your name
In you and you in us, we are one.
Help us to give
our lives to you,
As we live in
your love, as
we give up our
sins.
We love you,
Holy
Spirit.
We love
Each
Other
too,
It's all because of you.
It's 'just' because you
live in us all, who believe
in You,
Holy Spirit.
Thank You, Holy Spirit.
Thank you for your Peace.
Thank you for being so gentle with us.
May we be your instruments?
Holy Spirit, you are so good.
We confess we love you again, and again...
Holy Spirit, we speak to you.
We praise you and find you deep down inside of us.
We feel your presence, Holy Spirit.
Blessed be your name...
Amen...

The Grace We Seek: awareness of the reality of sin in the world.

It seems to me in the light of the Divine Goodness, although others may think differently, that ingratitude is the most abominable of sins and that it should be detested in the sight of our Creator and Lord by all of His creatures who are capable of enjoying His divine and everlasting glory. For it is a forgetting of the graces, benefits, and blessings received. As such it is the cause, beginning, and origin of all sins and misfortunes. On the contrary, the grateful acknowledgment of blessings and gifts received is esteemed not only on earth but in heaven.

Ignatius of Loyola, Letters of Saint Ignatius of Loyola

Week Eight

And a woman in the city, who was a sinner, having learned that he was eating in the Pharisee's house, brought an alabaster jar of ointment. She stood behind him at his feet, weeping, and began to bathe his feet with her tears and to dry them with her hair. And he said to the woman, "Your faith has saved you; go in peace."

Luke 7:37–38, 50

We wash other people's feet when we take care of the naked, hungry, and those in need, as opposed to merely wishing them well and going on our way. In Genesis, Cain asks God, "Am I my brother's keeper?" I believe the answer is yes. We are our brother's keeper. I think the woman who washed Jesus' feet knew this and her sins were forgiven. The call to wash the feet of the poor, the marginalised, and the stranger among us extends beyond national boundaries or rights of citizenship. We are called to see the face of God in all we encounter, and if we follow that call in our daily lives, the ramifications can be great indeed. How can I be angry at other drivers in traffic if I see the face of God in them? How can I hate someone of a different race or ethnicity if I see the face of God in them? And how can I exploit another country's resources or wage economic or physical war if the face of God is in those I oppose? Recognising and accepting that we see the face of God in all we encounter is the first step to following the Gospel of Peace.

Our focus is to become more aware of sin in the world created good by God, but has then fallen. We aim to realise our own personal failings and sins and by recognising our own sin, experience the grace and gift of God's unconditional love for us.

The Grace We Seek: understanding of how sin affects our own choices each day.

Without the willingness to be spiritually challenged, we cannot and will not change. Without the will to give up whatever is asked of us in order to meet a bigger God, we find that our understanding and experience of the Divine cannot and will not grow.
Paul Coutinho, How Big Is Your God?

Week Nine

Have mercy on me, O God, according to your steadfast love; according to your abundant mercy blot out my transgressions. Wash me thoroughly from my iniquity, and cleanse me from my sin. For I know my transgressions, and my sin is ever before me.
Psalms 51:1–3

During my Examen today, I concentrated on identifying, feeling, sharing, and enjoying God's presence in myself and others. It was a relatively quiet day, so I had more time to think about everything. As I filed a lot of sales files and folders, I realised again that I will soon be leaving the property I have worked so hard for so many years. The Indian Rivers Mental Health entity is going to make an offer to me on it next week. I will have to take it, if it is enough to adequately pay off my creditors. If not, I will have to declare bankruptcy. I really want to make the correct decisions about what to do the rest of my life. Promoting the Gospel of the Kingdom of God and the Gospel of Peace is now on top of my list.

I also considered the Examen that all mankind will eventually face at the resurrection. That Examen will consider what we did when we saw Jesus naked, hungry, and in need of our brothers and sisters. Did we feed Him (them) or not? This test is most especially relevant when those brothers and sisters are the least among us. What arc 'the Causes and Consequences of Sin'? What have I done to cause my own difficulties? May we to seek to understand and grow in the Graces of knowledge of how the world influences our own choices, how our decision to sin affects others in the world, the grace to become aware of our own disordered affections, which distance us from God, and to discover our own principle sins and the venial sins which stem from them. Finally, let us seek the grace of thanksgiving to God, for his forgiveness, mercy, and faithfulness.

The Grace We Seek: growing awareness of how our sins affect those around us.

This is what is meant by the famous Ignatian motto "finding God in all things". 'All things' to Ignatius is the whole panoply of human drama—our relationships, our work, our strivings and failures, our hopes and dreams. God can be found in all of it.
David L. Fleming, SJ, What Is Ignatian Spirituality?

Week Ten

Therefore, to keep me from being too elated, a thorn was given me in the flesh, a messenger of Satan to torment me, to keep me from being too elated. Three times I appealed to the Lord about this, that it would leave me, but he said to me, "My grace is sufficient for you, for power is made perfect in weakness." So, I will boast all the more gladly of my weaknesses, so that the power of Christ may dwell in me. Therefore I am content with weaknesses, insults, hardships, persecutions, and calamities for the sake of Christ; for whenever I am weak, then I am strong.

2 Corinthians 12:7–10

I learned this afternoon that my personal hand tools in Illinois, where I was helping the Amish and showing them how to hand cut dovetails, had been stolen from our farm shed. These are tools I have used for many years. Although they would not be worth a lot to put up for sale at auction, the replacement value would be multiple thousands of dollars. I wanted to keep them in case I needed to do manual cabinetwork again. Tomorrow is when the board of Indian Rivers Mental Health is to meet and consider purchasing my commercial property. There is a lot going on in my life. Maybe I can discern from all these things that God has other things in mind for me to do the rest of my life. I will keep trying to grow in an ever-deepening awareness of God's merciful love and an ever-greater gratitude for that mercy and love. A part of the Exercise now is to imagine our own lives as a house with rooms... We have unseemly rooms in our lives and in our houses, such as bathrooms and bedrooms. We want to invite our friends into our home in such cleaned up rooms as the living room, but to be realistic with God, we must invite God into all our rooms, to see all we are, and all we do, and to admit we are not perfect and we rely only on His grace and mercy.

The Grace We Seek: an ever-deepening awareness and appreciation of God's merciful love.

Are we responsible for our unmerited suffering? The answer is no. And yes. We are not responsible for our predicament as its cause—whether it be cancer or job loss or the death of a child or spouse. But we are responsible for what we do with the effects. For what we build comes from the rubble that fate has made of our lives.
William J. O' Malley, God: The Oldest Question

The Second Week
Week Eleven

O God, you are my God, I seek you
my soul thirsts for you;
my flesh faints for you,
as in a dry and weary land where there is no
water.
So I have looked upon you in the sanctuary,
beholding your power and glory.
Because your steadfast love is better than life,
my lips will praise you.
So I will bless you as long as I live;
I will lift up my hands and call on your name.
Psalm 63:1–2

I spent a whole day dealing with the theft of the mechanic and woodworking tools from the shed on my family farm. The tools that were originally mine, especially the woodworking tools, are a part of my identity. I collected and used many of them for over forty years. But I have been thinking more and more that my sense of identity needs some modification anyway. I am a cabinetmaker, but maybe that is not who I need to be for the rest of my life.

The goal is to channel the gratitude from my first week's experience into offering ourselves to God. We want to channel our desire for God into just what God wants for us in this life.

Mother Mary offered herself to God's desires for her:
Luke 1:46–55

46 And Mary said: "My soul glorifies the Lord
47 and my spirit rejoices in God my Saviour,
48 for he has been mindful of the humble state of.
49 From now on, all generations will call me blessed,
50 for the Mighty One has done great things for me—holy is his name.
51 His mercy extends to those who fear him, from generation to generation.
52 He has performed mighty deeds with his arm;He has scattered those who are proud in their inmost thoughts.
53 He has brought down rulers from their thrones but has lifted up the humble.
54 He has filled the hungry with good things but has sent the rich away empty.
55 He has helped his servant Israel, remembering to be merciful
56 to Abraham and his descendants forever, even as he said to our fathers."[4]

---

[4] Luke 1:46-55 - NIV

The Grace We Seek: the willingness to offer myself to fulfil God's will.

Man is created to praise, revere, and serve God, our Lord, and by this means to save his soul. The other things on the face of the earth are created to for man to help him in attaining the end for which he is created.

St. Ignatius of Loyola, The Spiritual Exercises

Week Twelve

I do not call you servants any longer, because the servant does not know what the master is doing; but I have called you friends, because I have made known to you everything that I have heard from my Father. You did not choose me but I chose you.

John 15:15–16

Early one morning while visiting my aunt in Illinois, I became aware of the different ways we pray. She was praying the Rosary that morning, while I was listening to what the Scriptures, the Word in writing, were saying to me. Silence can also be prayer. Our daily work can also be a form of prayer if we do it deliberately and with intention. No one way is the best, but different forms of prayer will facilitate our connection with God more effectively at different times in our lives. Here is a form of prayer I wrote, calling it my personal Magnificat. Maybe you would like to compose your own Magnificat too.

How Great!

How great is the Lord my God! He is beyond my understanding.
He has taken me not just from being a shepherd,
But from growing up the son of a poor farmer,
He has seen my every sin, and He still loves me.
He has satisfied my every need.
Even though I do not know what He is preparing me for,

Or how He will finish it,
I know the Lord has been good to me,
And will be good to me.
I know the Lord will raise me again,
And, I hope, will raise all humankind.
I give my concerns up to the Lord.
The Lord cares for my brothers and sisters;
For my wife, and for my spiritual family.
He sees every tear that falls from my face.
The Lord is good and I hope to dwell with Him
forever.

The Grace We Seek: to know Jesus more intimately, to love him more intensely, and to follow him more closely.

Ignatian spirituality is about being fully present to the moment, every moment, including those during prayer and those throughout the day. The depth of Ignatian prayer comes not from saying any particular words or incantation, but from being fully in a moment of relationship with Christ.

Margaret Silf, Inner Compass

Week Thirteen

For where your treasure is, there will your heart be also.

Matthew 6:21

Today was a pivotal day in my life. I finally received an offer on my property, and it was less than half of what I was hoping for. Unless something changes, or I make a radically higher counter offer and it is accepted, this means bankruptcy for me. I know that God will provide, but I am realising how much I am concerned by the things I store up...

The Grace We Seek: to let go of those attachments that do not lead us to God.

The maxim of illusory religion runs: "Fear not; trust in God and He will see that none of the things you fear will happen to you"; that of real religion, on the contrary, is "Fear not; the things that you are afraid of are quite likely to happen to you, but they are nothing to be afraid of."

John Macmurray, Persons in Relation

Week Fourteen

And this is my prayer, that your love may overflow more and more with knowledge and full insight to help you determine what is best.

Philippians 1:9–10

Today, Robert, who used to work with us, came in to pack up some imported cabinets, perhaps the last job we will ship out of our warehouse. He did a good job and I helped him remember how to do things. I have employed a lot of people and I have helped a lot of people. Perhaps my job in this field is done, and God has other things for me to do. I wish I knew. I feel I am in a phase of waiting. I stand ready for God to do with me as God will.

The Grace We Seek: to trust in God's will for our lives.

Knowing that we can trust our experience is the first, and perhaps the most fundamental, lesson about discernment. We can discern the right direction by thoughtful reflection on our relationships with others, our work in the world, and on the feelings those encounters generated. They are meaningful because God is in them.

J. Michael Sparough, SJ, What's Your Decision?

Week Fifteen

And he said to them, "Follow me, and I will make you fish for people." Immediately they left their nets and followed him.

Matthew 4:19–20

What have I done for Christ today? We all have the same twenty-four hours per day to choose how much time we are going to give back to God, how much time we want to live only in God's love and grace. We all must choose our ways to follow Christ. I choose to follow the Gospel of Peace—to be a living example of non-violence as Jesus preached; to lay down the sword of intolerance, anger, and hatred; to see the face of God in all I encounter.

The Grace We Seek: to listen to and perform what Christ wants for us.

To discover what we deeply, truly desire forces us to wade into a swamp of needs, expectations, demands, casual wishes, moods, obligations, and much more. Your deepest, truest desire may coincide with one or another of these interior experiences but will always cut deeper into your heart than any of them... These deepest, truest desires constitute and reveal a person's core identity.

George A. Aschenbrenner, SJ, Stretched for Greater Glory

Week Sixteen

Let the words of my mouth and the meditation of my heart be acceptable to you, O Lord, my rock and my redeemer.

Psalm 19:14

I turned the lights off and imagined Jesus as a young man, as I once was. I imagined Jesus and I working together to build the chest of drawers that my great-great-grandfather, Alexander Hinkle, built. The chest, which I inherited, is made out of cherry and has hand-cut dovetails and markings of hand tools used in the mid-1800s. I imagine that Jesus mainly used hand tools and this is one way He increased in strength. Working with Jesus is fun. Jesus works hard. I also think about how, regardless of our trade, we can work as if Jesus is right here, right now, working with us. Oh, we are building two chests, one chest for Mother Mary, and another one for Mary Magdalene.

Continuing in my quest to grow closer to Jesus and to follow Him more nearly, my thoughts and prayers focus upon Joseph, Jesus' father. I did not actually open the Bible as I did before to read the story. Instead, I found just a couple of songs on *YouTube*, like 'Joseph's Song', by Michael Card.[5] There are not many songs about Joseph I could find. There is not much in the Bible regarding Joseph. I want to ask a couple of my male friends, Keith Watson being one, about raising an adopted child. I imagine Joseph being a kind and just person, a hard worker, and a skilled

---

[5] See: https://www.youtube.com/watch?v=H6onryQfuCQ

businessman. I imagine he silently bore the stigma of being a father out of wedlock but was comforted by the times the Angels spoke directly to him, guiding him in what He should do and how He should help protect the growing child, Jesus, that the fallen angels would probably have liked to have killed. I recall that after Jesus was found in the Temple that Jesus grew in stature with God and man and was obedient to His parents. I can imagine Joseph teaching Jesus His trade. I have taught many people cabinet making. The song referred to Joseph as a 'simple carpenter'. There is nothing 'simple' about being a carpenter or a cabinetmaker or working in stone. I imagine him as a deeply spiritual person, perhaps with access to the temple scrolls due to his illustrious lineage. I think this because I think Jesus must have had early access to the Scriptures of His day, and perhaps He read them together with Joseph. Maybe Jesus had a photographic memory and was gifted with a high IQ, as well as being fully God which must help matters out a lot. I imagine Joseph was an intelligent man too, and a just man.

The heart of the Examen prayer is:

What Have I Done for Christ?
What am I Doing for Christ?
What Should I Do for Christ?

What have I done for Christ today? I think, for one thing, I devoted some time to Him in prayer and meditation. We can often tell what we do and our priorities by how we spend our time. Another thing I did is to pick up the book Sr. Madeleine gave me to read, *The Imitation of Christ* by Thomas á Kempis,[6] and read just a little that I feel I should share. It is from Chapter 20: Of Love, of Solitude, and Silence: "If you will withdraw yourself from superfluous words and from unprofitable business, and from hearing rumours and idle tales, you will find convenient time to be occupied in holy meditation."

I stopped right there – I needed to let that soak in a while... Literally speaking, if I had withdrawn myself from my unprofitable business when the recession hit, instead of spending so much now having to withdraw in possible bankruptcy, I would perhaps be better off. But I did not know then what I know now, and the meaning of the text is not literal business, although it could be, but such business as seeking pleasure before seeking God. At any rate, we all have the same twenty-four hours per day to choose how much time we are going to give back to God, how much time we want to live only in His love and grace. Tomorrow, what I think I should do is to evaluate what time I have and how to best use it. I am nearly sixty-six years old[7] and

---

[6] See: http://www.traditionalcatholicpriest.com/wp-content/uploads/2015/09/imitation.pdf.

[7] To put this edit in a time frame, I was born January 15th, 1949, and apparently wrote this section of the original journal notes just after Christmas, 2015, when I was doing the Exercises. As I edit today, January 14th, 2019,

I should have been thinking about such things long ago. I think that is why I have been led to these St. Ignatian Spiritual Exercises. One of the things we should do for Christ is to give Him some time in reflections and meditations.

The Grace We Seek: the awareness that Jesus seeks a deep and meaningful friendship with us.

People say, "I become distracted whenever I try to pray." My response to this is to suggest that people make the distraction the content of their prayer, to hear God's word in this person, situation, whatever it might be. It is usually the very situation or person that we should be thinking, reflecting, praying about in the presence of the Lord. So I think most of the distractions we get are really not distractions.

J.J. O'Leary, SJ,
Finding God in All Things: A Marquette Prayer Book

almost seventy years old. Time continues to flow, and the sooner in life one dedicates oneself to God, to knowing Him more clearly, to following him more nearly, and loving Him more nearly, the better it is for oneself and everyone else too. It is never too late and it is never too early. Now is the time. I believe this book, as far as I am aware, is unique in presenting Ignatian Spirituality as an actual human experience in life, sharing what I have lost, not merely an intellectual outline to be followed, although I attempt to make the Exercises as easily followed as possible. Still, working with a Spiritual Director in companionship with a small group is, I believe, the best way to do the Exercises.

Week Seventeen

The farmer waits for the precious crop from the earth, being patient with it until it receives the early and the late rains. You also must be patient.

James 5:7–8

I think I experienced a little identity crisis today. I was bidding on *eBay* for some antique dovetail saws, thinking I would at least like to replace the tools I need to hand-cut dovetails. I am about to go bankrupt, and I do not really have any money to replace my stolen tools, and no one is going to pay me for hand-cut dovetails, but I tried to get them anyway. I am supposed to accept being crucified with Christ and giving up my old identity and yielding to the new inner man in me. I need to concentrate on is what is useful for discerning what I am offering to Christ at nearly sixty-six years old, not what once was. I do not know what the future holds for me, but I don't think it is going to be cutting hand-cut dovetails.

Speaking of identity, who is Jesus in my imagination to me? I spent time imagining what Jesus may have looked like. I have long rejected the blue-eyed, white-skinned Jesus in favour of a darker-skinned person more typical of the region and time. After all, He had to be pointed out by Judas to the Roman guards. I imagine He had strong arms and hands from working in wood with hand tools and lifting heavy beams and stones. I do not think His hair would have been unusually long for His day, and I do not think He would necessarily have had a beard, but He may have. What does He look like now?

I imagine Jesus' ancestors were from all over the place on the genetic map coming down from Judah. I think normally when one does genealogy, one leaves out the 'bad' side, and in Jewish culture one also leaves out the 'women' too. But that's not what Matthew does… He lists Tamar[8] who had a child by her stepfather under the table, so to speak, Rahab,[9] a Canaanite and a prostitute, and Ruth,[10] a Moabite, and of course, Bathsheba,[11] someone else's wife.

See Public Domain Art depicting Tamar, and links below for others in Jesus' lineage.

[12]

---

[8] https://en.wikipedia.org/wiki/Tamar_(Genesis)
[9] https://en.wikipedia.org/wiki/Rahab
[10] https://en.wikipedia.org/wiki/Ruth_(biblical_figure)
[11] https://en.wikipedia.org/wiki/Bathsheba
[12] *Judah and Tamar*, Horace Vernet

The Grace We Seek: to know who we are and imagine we can be like Jesus

Usually, it's quite difficult to sort out the confusing muddle of ordered and disordered attachments that most of us live with. We begin to answer these difficult questions by starting from a point of freedom—detachment from any particular outcome, from other people's ideas of the good life, from considerations of how someone like you should act.

Jim Manney, God Finds Us

Horace Vernet – The Yorck Project: *10.000 Meisterwerke der Malerei.* DVD-ROM, 2002. ISBN 3936122202. Distributed by DIRECTMEDIA Publishing GmbH.

Interlude

We are about half way through our book and it is a good time for us to pause and consider our calling. Has anything so far given you a new and different experience of who God is to you? Who is Jesus to you? Is He just a man descended from His ancestors? In the Exercises, Ignatius wants us to consider what he calls 'The Call of Christ the King'. We are advised at the outset that this extra-biblical exercise designed by St. Ignatius, who had pursued vanity and glory as a soldier in his life, will need some 'translation' since he created it from his point of view as a warrior who devoted himself to following the standard, or banner, of his feudal king. We are to imagine a human King, chosen by God, whom all Christian Princes and people revere and obey. This reminds me of the Old Testament story in which God told Samuel that the people had not rejected Samuel, but God, in their desire for a King, and all the bad things that would happen if Israel chose this type of governance system.

I quote below from *The Spiritual Exercises of St. Ignatius*, by Ludovico J. Puhl, SJ, regarding the Grace we desire in this Exercise:

91. *The Kingdom of Christ*
The Call of an Earthly King
This will help us to contemplate the life of the eternal king
Prayer. The preparatory prayer will be as usual.

First Prelude: This is a mental representation of the place. Here it will be to see in imagination the

synagogues, villages, and towns where Christ, our
Lord, preached.

Second Prelude: I will ask for the grace I desire.
Here it will be to ask of our Lord the grace not to be
deaf to His call, but prompt and diligent to accomplish
His most holy will.

This exercise is about Christ, the King. If I had to
choose a human king, it would be Pope Francis, the
current leader of the Vatican State. From the time I
first sensed who he was as a human being, I
immediately sensed a spiritual connection with him as
his mission became clear, to rectify the corruption in
the Catholic Church, and to carry the Gospel to the
whole world. After all, he chose 'Francis' as his papal
name, after St. Francis of Assisi who responded to
Christ's calling to "Go, rebuild my Church which is
falling down" through prayer, poverty, and peace. As a
result of Pope Francis's message, I have even
entertained the idea of attending the Catholic Church
again, to see how his calling from Christ the King is
working out. I have returned at times, but I do not feel
the call of Christ the King to return to full communion
with the Church. But this human king, Pope Francis,
comes to us in allegiance to the Beatitudes. He urges
us to follow the King who came to serve, to be a
peacemaker, and to accept poverty of spirit and to look
like Jesus, whose instructions for His Kingdom were
for us to serve each other in love.

Are there people in the world today whom you
might choose to be your human king, whose lives are
examples of peace, mercy, humility, and love? We
should be careful not to put our faith into any one man
or woman, but rather into the message they bring,
because it is in the message we can find Christ.

To know Jesus as our King, to know Jesus more
intimately, to love him more intensely, and to follow

him more closely, let us focus on poverty, spiritual poverty and/or actual physical poverty, and utter dependence upon God. In prayer with Matthew 4:1–11, Jesus' period of fasting in preparation for His public ministry, I realised that Jesus had to face the same temptations that all other human beings face, even at the height of the gifts of spiritual riches we receive after periods of meditation and prayer. Some of the temptations Jesus faced were that of conceit and pride, areas in which Satan was testing Jesus. Just show how good you are Jesus, Satan whispered, to turn stones into bread, to jump off high walls like the superman that you really are. You are so deserving. Just take over all the kingdoms of the earth – now, you do not have to really die.

How are we sometimes tempted in similar ways? Are there ways in which we attempt to turn stone into bread? Do we sometimes presume to know God's mind and therefore benefit from God's protection? Does our ambition ever cloud our judgement?

Paul warns us against conceit and pride in his letter to the Galatians chapter 5, where he lists some of the gifts of the Spirit and cautions us not to be conceited. I have faced these temptations of conceit and pride all my life and for way too many years I have succumbed to them in opposition to living simply with spiritual gifts and living in spiritual poverty in utter and complete dependence on God, and not on myself. I think the early church faced these temptations too. For example, in the time of Constantine, the church was presented with power, political power over actual physical kingdoms of the earth and the church accepted, becoming the church, Militant and Triumphant, physically, not spiritually speaking – caving in to the temptation of Satan. I am disenfranchised from political systems, but still face the temptations of conceit and pride. At least I am aware of the problem and finally know I must resist the temptations.

Regarding the second temptation of Jesus, at least the second one according to the Gospel of Matthew, Jesus was taken to the highest point of the Temple and asked to jump off because the angels had charge over him and would bear him up lest he cast a foot against the ground according to the scripture Satan quoted. However, Jesus quoted another scripture, "You shall not tempt (or test) the Lord your God."

These temptations are allowed in preparation for Jesus' proclaiming of the Good News of the Kingdom of God. It takes discernment when one is placed in high positions to recognise who has put one in the position and if it is to serve God's greater purposes or one's own self-aggrandisement. It would have looked very good to others if Jesus could fly off the building and if angels were to catch Him. What a wonderful person, everyone would say, a real 'superman'!

Ignatius asks us to consider which king we will serve, under which standard (flag on a pole) we will stand. Will it be the standard of Jesus one can imagine Jesus held high at the Sermon on the Mount? Will it be the standard of Satan?

"The Two Standards"

The Two Standards (imagine flags) contain the core of the Spiritual Exercises and are the major reason I was initially attracted to St. Ignatius. They tell us how to make lifetime and daily decisions to follow Jesus in our lives. In some ways, I had discovered some of these principles in my life already. Let's concentrate in meditations on the instructions of the exercise only, without consulting Scripture. I believe the concepts of the Two Standards as explained in the *Exercises* are not based upon specific scriptural references, as given by St. Ignatius, but they could be. I imagine Jesus on the Sermon on the Mount setting the standard and holding the standard high for all to see of who God really is, the God who actually loves His enemies, does good to those who despitefully uses Him, and blesses those who curse Him. This is the nonviolent Jesus who raises this standard. This is the God of peace. The Two Standards portrays a choice of standing under the banner of God, or the banner of Satan. Or the way of 'give' as opposed to the way of 'get', or the Kingdom of God as opposed to the Kingdoms of the world is a way of speaking of the Two Standards that makes a lot of sense to me. The discernment of realising just who's standard or banner one stands under in every area of life is crucial to proper living in Christ. The Grace we desire is an awareness of the enemy's deceits and for courage and confidence in the face of those deceits to understand God's way of living and have a heartfelt desire to live God's Way.

One of the things one may consider is the area of inordinate attachments. I have already come to a realisation of some of my own vanity and pride over the past few years and have been doing spiritual battle with those beasts. I have also begun to understand the beast of inordinate attachments that is mentioned in this exercise. I have in the past been and sometimes I still am, standing under Satan's standard in desire of riches and success. Maybe God allowed my most cherished personal hand tools to be stolen to help release me from that inordinate attachment. Tools are fine if one needs them, and God wants one to work with them. I suppose it is OK to like them, but, I know I need to release all things to God and cling only to Him in these steps of self-purification needed to stand under God's standard or banner in preparation for service in the Kingdom of God, now and forever. Do you have any disordinate attachments you could give up?

As we leave this interlude and consideration of Christ, the King, and the Two Standards, of the Spiritual Exercises, we are now asking for the Grace to grow in interior freedom so we can respond wholeheartedly to Christ's motivation in our lives. We must realise that choosing to stand under the standard of Christ involves Solidarity with the poor, and with sinners too. Just how many of the poor, and how many known to be 'sinners', beside ourselves, that is, do we know and love? Do we talk and walk with the poor, or our enemies? Do we drink out of the same well as others who are needy, or provide them with the drink they need?

One more thing about the Two Standards, when I originally wrote the manuscript for this book, Kayla Mueller was in the news. She chose the correct standard of Christ the King. Kayla was an American girl of about 25 years' old who has devoted her life to helping refugees and was captured by ISIS, the terrorist organisation. I am including her letter as an example that choosing the correct standard does not guarantee a long and carefree life: it may be just the opposite. Here is her letter, in Kayla's memory:

Everyone, if you are receiving this letter it means I am still detained but my cellmates (starting from 11/2/2014) have been released. I have asked them to contact you + send you this letter. It's hard to know what to say. Please know that I am in a safe location, completely unharmed + healthy (put on weight in fact): I have been treated w/ the utmost respect + kindness. I wanted to write you all a well-thought-out letter (but I didn't know if my cell mates would be leaving in the coming days or the coming months restricting my time but primarily) I could only but write the letter a paragraph at a time, just the thought of you all sends me into a fit of tears. If you could say I have 'suffered' at all throughout this whole experience it is only in knowing how much suffering I have put you all through: I will never ask you to forgive me as I do not deserve forgiveness. I remember mom always telling me that all in all in the end the only one you really have is God. I have come to a place in experience where, in every sense of the word, I have surrendered myself to our creator b/c literally there was no one else… + by God + by your prayers I have felt tenderly cradled in freefall. I have been shown in darkness, light + have learned that in every situation, sometimes we just have to look for it. I pray each day that if nothing else, you have felt a certain closeness + surrender to God as well + have formed a bond of love + support amongst each other… I miss you all as if it has been a decade of forced separation. I have had many a long hour to think, to think of all the things I will do w/ Lex, our first camping trip, the first meeting @ the airport. I have had many hours to think how only in your absence have I finally @ 25 years old come to realise your place in my life. The gift that is each one of you + the person I could + could not be if you were not a part of my life, my family, my support. I DO NOT want the negotiations for my release to be your duty, if there is your burden. I have asked these women to support you: please seek their advice. If you have not done so already. [REDACTED] can contact [REDACTED] who may have a certain level of experience with these people. None of us could have known it would be this long but know I am also fighting from my side in the ways I am able + I have a lot of fight left inside of me. I am not breaking down + I will not give in no matter how long it takes. I wrote a song some months ago that says, "The part of me that pains the most also gets me out of bed, w/out your hope there would be nothing left…" aka – The thought of your pain is the source of my own, simultaneously the hope of our reunion is the source of my strength. Please be patient, give your pain to God. I know you would want me to remain strong. That is exactly what I am doing. Do not fear for me, continue to pray as will I + by God's will we will be together soon.

All my everything. Kayla[13, 14]

[13] see: http://www.independent.co.uk/news/world/middle-east/kayla-mueller-full-transcript-of-letter-sent-by-usaid-worker-held-hostage-by-isis-10036557.html
[14]see:http://www.nytimes.com/interactive/2015/02/10/world/middleeast/document-kayla-muellers-letterfrom-captivity.html?_r=0

Week Eighteen

Even though we speak in this way, beloved, we are confident of better things in your case, things that belong to salvation. For God is not unjust; he will not overlook your work and the love that you showed for his sake in serving the saints, as you still do.

Hebrews 6:9–10

I will most likely officially file bankruptcy this week, and I have been thinking about how things might have gone differently. The recession has been going on for years and the housing market has been especially hard hit, but perhaps I tried to hang on for too long, relying on borrowed money after our reserves ran out. I was not drawing a salary myself but tried to keep my staff together for quite a while after the company began losing money. I have been thinking about all the people I have employed and my dreams for my business that will never come to happen. I have worked so hard, perhaps not always wisely and not always completely for others, but I have done much in God's service and for my employees and for my customers that I believe will not be forgotten as I make a transition in life to I do not know what.

The Grace We Seek: the willingness to wholeheartedly accept Christ's invitation in our lives

Wisdom is making peace with the unchangeable. We have the freedom to face the unavoidable with dignity, to understand the transformational value that attitude works on suffering. We are not responsible for

our predicament as its cause—whether it be cancer or job loss or the death of a child or spouse. But we are responsible for what we do with the effects, for what we build from the rubble that fate has made of our lives.

    William O'Malley, SJ, God: The Oldest Question

Week Nineteen

Therefore do not worry, saying, 'What will we eat?' or 'What will we drink?' or 'What will we wear?' For it is the Gentiles who strive for all these things; and indeed your heavenly Father knows that you need all these things. But strive first for the kingdom of God and his righteousness, and all these things will be given to you as well.

Matthew 6:31–33

As part of the Spiritual Exercises, I am carefully considering my inordinate attachments. I have already come to a realisation of some of my own vanity and pride over the past few years and have been doing spiritual battle with those beasts. I have in the past been, and sometimes I still am, standing under Satan's standard in desire of riches and success. I wonder if God allowed my most cherished personal hand tools to be stolen to help release me from that inordinate attachment. Tools are fine if one needs them, and God wants one to work with them, but I know I need to release all things to God and cling only to Him in these steps of self-purification needed to stand under God's standard or banner in preparation for service in the Kingdom of God, now and forever. We can give up our attachments, our addictions, and fall in Love with God. Let us consider this poem:

Fall in Love

Nothing is more practical than finding God,
that is, than falling in love
in a quite absolute, final way.

What you are in love with,
what seizes your imagination,
will affect everything.

It will decide what will get you out of bed in the
morning,
what you will do with your evenings,
how you will spend your weekends,
what you read,
who you know,
what breaks your heart,
and what amazes you with joy and gratitude.

Fall in love,
stay in love,
and it will decide everything.
By: Fr. Pedro Arrupe, SJ

We have to decide who we are going to love. The process of Ignatian discernment is about deciding between good things. For example, a young adult who has been accepted to more than one college may choose to use Ignatian discernment to determine the right option and how he/she can use their choice to better serve God's will. Someone who has come into a large sum of money may use Ignatian discernment to help them decide how best to spend that money. In fact, Ignatius presents this very scenario in the *Exercises* in a section called the 'Three Classes of Men'. He asks us to consider three types of people and how each would respond to sudden wealth, if it would enslave them or if they would have interior freedom to still serve God according to God's desire for them and their particular calling. Each of the three men had received a large sum of money. One wanted to give it all away immediately, so he would not be attached to it. Another wanted to keep it but be sure he had given away any attachment to the money. The third wanted to reach a state of 'holy indifference' so that he would only want God's will for him, to retain no attachment for the money nor the desire to keep it, but only to do what God wanted with it.

What then, are our deepest desires? If you were to go on an Ignatian retreat, you may be asked, "What do you want?" Every retreat is likely to be a different experience. I asked myself before going to my last retreat, "What do I want?" This time I wanted to rest in God's presence and listen for Him to speak. Perhaps you, the reader, should stop now and ask in prayer:

What do I want?

What are your innermost desires? Have you discovered a sixth sense that is built into you before you were born to taste and see the things of God? Could you desire union with God more than anything else? Could you give up everything to live in the love and grace of God? Could you fall in love with Him so that nothing else matters and if He were to ask you to take only the clothes you are wearing now, one pair of sandals, and a walking stick to go about town and other cities, with no money or food? (See Mark 6).

The Three Classes of Men is about our desires, our addictions to not just money, but to our self. Humility is a key to discerning how this parable applies to each of us. One must ask for the grace we desire to choose wisely what God wants for us in our lives. What God wants for us is likely to change at various points in our lives, but always we should want to give up our self-will to use whatever we have and whomever we are for the praise and worship and service of God. We can do this through God's grace. His grace alone can release our self and ego from attachments and addictions so we come to a state of 'passionate indifference', which is to want only what God wants for us.

Which path to choose?
Jessica Powers: Repairer of fences

I am alone in the dark, and I am thinking
what darkness would be mine if I could see
the ruin I wrought in every place I wandered
and if I could not be
aware of One who follows after me.
Whom do I love, O God, when I love Thee?
The great Undoer who has torn apart
the walls I built against a human heart,
the Mender who has sewn together the hedges
through which I broke when I went seeking ill,
the Love who follows and forgives me still.
Fumbler and fool that I am, with things around me
Of fragile make like souls, how I am blessed
To hear behind me footsteps of a Saviour!
I sing to the east; I sing to the west:
God is my repairer of fences, turning my paths into
rest.

The Grace We Seek: the freedom to follow Christ more closely, walking stick and all we are and will become.

Understanding personal attachments means overturning personal rocks to see what crawls out. Attachment to money is usually salve for some other debilitating ego-itch: I'm terrified of failing; I need to feel important and be the centre of attention; I'm insecure about my real talent and worth. This is what

Loyola was really after: the internal fears, drives, and attachments that can control decisions and actions.

Chris Lowney, Heroic Leadership

Week Twenty

"Let the little children come to me; do not stop them; for it is to such as these that the kingdom of God belongs. Truly I tell you, whoever does not receive the kingdom of God as a little child will never enter it."

Mark 10:14–15

I am beginning to listen to the inner movements of the Spirit and discern what is happening. I thought today about how my financial difficulties have really helped my spiritual growth. They have helped me to trust God. They have helped to reduce my conceit and pride. I am also beginning to understand spiritual poverty and my need to completely rely on God for everything that brings life and salvation. I am learning not to be so quick to think that I know best about matters related to religion and theology. I am still sorting all these things out and still learning.

The Grace We Seek: the fortitude to serve God and others.

Humility says, "How can I serve you?"
Hubris says, "Here's how you fix yourself."
Greg Boyle, SJ

Week Twenty-One

"But love your enemies, do good, and lend, expecting nothing in return. Your reward will be great, and you will be children of the Most High; for he is kind to the ungrateful and the wicked. Be merciful, just as your Father is merciful."

Luke 6:35–36

It is hard for me to believe, actually, but apparently this is the road to take. I feel God has been with me as I have struggled the past few years. I think this is nothing new for believers to do, to face difficulties and trials. More and more, I trust God. Tomorrow is another day to trust God. It is never too late in life to hear, listen to, and heed Christ's calling. We are not all called to sell everything we have and do the exact same Kingdom-oriented endeavour, but we are all called to believe Jesus, and 'do' something.

The Grace We Seek: the openness to hear and follow Christ's call.

The self-giving God of Ignatian spirituality works within the universe, with human hearts and lives, giving men and women the strength to give of themselves.

Ronald Modras, Ignatian Humanism

Week Twenty-Two

"But I say to you that listen, love your enemies, do good to those who hate you, bless those who curse you, pray for those who abuse you. If anyone strikes you on the cheek, offer the other also."

Luke 6:27–29

Jesus already has a place ready for us in His Kingdom. He has a place that fulfils our dreams. He has a place where swords are beaten into plowshares. He has a place where there is a banquet table set out for the poor and starving in the world. He has a place where the rich are made low, and a place where the low are made rich. There is no need to want in this Kingdom of God's grace and peace. The vision and dreams God has for each of us are fulfilled in the ways we have already dreamed. God was there all along to see, to feel, and to hear each of our dreams. He is always with us to fulfil everything in the future and even the present. God has hopes and dreams for us we do not know yet.

Do we have a place for those in need in our own kingdoms, in our own nations and lives? I wondered about these matters and a Prayer of Imagination came to me:

A Prayer of Imagination
Little Boy

After a little while, Jesus went to a town called Nain with His apprentices and a great big crowd following Him. Nain is a town just off the beach in Greece and a little dead boy had just washed up on the beach. There was a war going on in Syria and his mother and the little boy had fled their home after the boy's father had been killed by a bombing raid on a hospital. The mother and child desperately wanted to be safe and embarked on a dangerous journey by sea to Greece. Their boat capsized, however, and the boy drowned while his mother only barely made it to the shore alive. Now that his body had been recovered, they were having a funeral for the little boy who was the woman's only child. The little boy was all she had left on earth. She had spent every penny she had on the little wood casket. She had no money for flowers.

Jesus saw the funeral procession and the woman crying and Jesus cried too. "It just is not right," Jesus muttered in between tears as He went up to the coffin and felt the smooth wood. The coffin was 5/4" thick cypress. Jesus was a carpenter and He had made some similar to this one before. It had hand-cut dovetail joints. Even though tears were coming out of Jesus' eyes, He told the woman, "Don't cry," and as He opened up the lid of the coffin, He said, "Little Boy, get up, I tell you". The little boy got up and started talking and Jesus helped him get out of the coffin,

holding his little body in His arms. He gave the little
boy back to his mother.

Everybody was filled with awe and they praised
God, even though not all of them were Christians.
Some of these refugees were Muslims and some were
Christians too, but they all praised God. "A great
prophet has appeared among us," they said. "God has
come to save His people."

Someone recorded the event on their cell phone
and posted it online for all to see just how much Jesus
loved the little boy and how much He cared for the
plight of the refugees. Because of this mystical and
mighty event, the whole world abstained from war for
forty-nine days.

The revision of the Gospel story from Luke 7:11–
17 is essentially a prayer of my imagination. This
prayer came to me as my state of active meditation and
contemplation slipped into a state of passive
contemplation.

The Grace We Seek: the courage to work for
justice and mercy for others.

Instead of loving what you think is peace, love
other men, and love God above all. And instead of
hating the people you think are warmongers, hate the
appetites and the disorder in your own soul, which are
the causes of war. If you love peace, then hate
injustice, hate tyranny, hate greed—but hate these
things in yourself, not in another.

Thomas Merton, Passion for Peace: Reflections on
War and Nonviolence

The Third Week
Week Twenty-Three

"And can any of you by worrying add a single hour to your span of life? If then you are not able to do so small a thing as that, why do you worry about the rest?"

Luke 12:25–26

I awoke very early this morning, about 3 AM and tried to get back to sleep, but could not. This is the day of bankruptcy. I thought in this early rising of the night before Jesus' crucifixion and how He was up all-night praying. Bankruptcy has been a long time coming as I have been trying to pay off my debts by selling the property I own. I could not sell it. The way I view it, I am forgiven of my debts. Likewise, I must be sure to forgive others as well. Forgiveness is a trade-off. Even financial forgiveness costs those who issue credit. Also, if one makes a profit, the profit one makes costs someone else. There is always the other side of the trade. The forgiveness of Jesus cost Him suffering too. Our sins are likewise costly, causing us to suffer. My sins have been forgiven, and therefore I must and I do release the sins of others against me.

Today's reflections begin 'week' 3, entitled 'The Passion of Christ'. I read Mark, Chapters 14–15, getting a preliminary view of what Jesus went through for us in His final hours. The grace for which we are asking is to learn Christ's call by walking with Him to Calvary, to be with him in his passion and death. From the Spiritual Exercises, (SpEx 193) we find it put this way:

(193) "Third Prelude: This is to ask for what I desire. Here it will be to ask for sorrow, compassion, and shame because the Lord is going to His suffering for my sins."[15]

Let us imagine we are we are right there with Jesus, feeling his inner turmoil, knowing we are facing death along with him, allowing ourselves the sorrow and pain he felt, feeling his tears, his sense of shock, knowing that this is it, the moment has arrived, and sensing the love He shared on his march to death, in companionship and love with his Father.

Another Grace We Seek: the freedom of indifference so that we may more truly perform God's will.

Do what you can calmly and gently. Do not be disturbed about the rest, but leave to God's providence what you cannot manage yourself. God is well pleased with the earnestness and moderate anxiety with which we attend to our obligations, but He is not pleased with that anxiety which afflicts the soul, because He wishes our limitations and weakness to seek the support of His strength and omnipotence, with the trust that in His goodness He will supply what is lacking to our weakness and shortcomings.

St. Ignatius of Loyola, The Letters of St. Ignatius of Loyola

---

[15]http://spex.ignatianspirituality.com/SpiritualExercises/P uhl#c19–1234

Week Twenty-Four

For I am convinced that neither death, nor life, nor angels, nor rulers, nor things present, nor things to come, nor powers, nor height, nor depth, nor anything else in all creation, will be able to separate us from the love of God in Christ Jesus, our Lord.

Romans 8:38–39

I am becoming more and more comfortable with the truth that I am God's beloved son, invited to His banquet table, to God's party where my feet are washed and anointed and I sit enjoying His presence. I was a cabinetmaker. I can still 'do' that, but a cabinetmaker is not who I am, really, it is what I do or have done. Now if someone asks who I am, in my heart I know I am, God's son. It might now be wise in some circumstances to not put it exactly like that, but that is my primary identity. Whatever our professions are today will not be needed for the eternal Kingdom of God as much as the transcendent truth of being beloved sons and daughters of God.

The Grace We Seek: solidarity with Christ's suffering.

Picture is Public Domain.

We are learning Christ's call by walking with Him to Calvary, being with Him in His Passion and death. I think about the central tool, the cross, to the message of the Gospel. I think about the message of Jesus, the Gospel of the Kingdom; the Gospel of Peace and of Salvation for all Mankind as being contained on the Cross and its meaning to us as Christians. I think about Jesus who cried out to the Father, "Father, forgive them for they know not what they do. Jesus was displayed His love for all of us on the cross, and the Father could not look on at the last moments...Eli, Eli, Lama Sabbactani, Jesus cried out of His humanity as if

He thought and as if we sometimes think God has forsaken Him, But God has not God loves us so much that He died for us on this cross. Father, forgive them – my friends and my enemies, so must we who are forgiven forgive our friends and enemies and share this Gospel of Peace and this call to a new Kingdom of Grace and love, of loving Jesus more dearly, of following Him more nearly, of knowing Him more clearly, turn the eyes on the cross."

When I ask what is certain for me in life and death, knowing that everything else may be anchored in it, the answer is the love of God as known in the heart of Christ.

Gary Smith, SJ, Radical Compassion…

Week Twenty-Five

Humble yourselves therefore under the mighty hand of God, so that he may exalt you in due time. Cast all your anxiety on him, because he cares for you.
1 Peter 5:6–738–39

Jesus' primary desire is for us to be participants in divine love. It is Love for the Father, love for the son, given us by the Holy Spirit, and shared with each other that Jesus wants us to understand as the heart of His message. It is a new commandment, to love one another as Jesus loved us, not an additional commandment to the Ten Commandments, not an additional commandment to the law which we are not under, but a commandment whereby we give up the old commandments and embrace the way of love that Jesus is pleading for us to understand as the only way.

The Grace We Seek: the willingness to be present with others as they experience suffering.

The God we are seeking to cooperate with is a God who is involved in every nook and cranny of the world, in its hellholes and its mini-paradises. Where do I choose to give my time and my attention and my energy, and from what do I choose to withdraw them? In Ignatian terms, and apostolically oriented spirituality demands that I learn how to live and act as a discerner of spirits and as a seeker of God's desire for me.
Brian McDermott, SJ, "What is Apostolic Spirituality?" America

Week Twenty-Six

Do nothing from selfish ambition or conceit, but in humility regard others as better than yourselves. Let each of you look not to your own interests, but to the interests of others. Let the same mind be in you that was in Christ Jesus.

Philippians 2:3–5

I think I am beginning to understand that doing these Examens—what we have done for Christ, what we are doing for Christ, and what we ought to do for Christ—is not so much about matters of great heroic feats or gigantic intellectual concepts but just presenting our bodies as willing vessels of Christ's love, if and when He chooses to use us as His tool. Our work is our service. At one point today, I stopped to read some letters from my mother when she was confined to a nursing home from 1981–1983 and wept as I remembered her and the pain and suffering she went through. Yet she was always concerned for her children and painfully wrote thank you letters with her arthritic fingers. I was inspired to call a friend in the nursing home who recently had a stroke. It turned out to be a good day to speak to him and his wife. Tomorrow, let me just present myself as a vessel of the love of Christ.

The Grace We Seek: to have sorrow, compassion, and empathy for the suffering of others.

How do you 'know' if you have found God in a moment of your day? For me, it is like hitting a hard reset on my computer; it is reconnecting to my mission, to that which makes me tick and makes seek goodness. It is the self-awareness of seeing what is truly important and needed in a situation rather than just what I want. It is the moment of gratitude for what is, and the release of the angst for what isn't.

Lisa Kelly, This Ignatian Life blog

The Fourth Week
Week Twenty-Seven

Come to me, all you that are weary and are carrying heavy burdens, and I will give you rest. Take my yoke upon you, and learn from me; for I am gentle and humble in heart, and you will find rest for your souls. For my yoke is easy, and my burden is light.
Matthew 11:28–30

What does it mean that Jesus will go before the disciples into Galilee? Where is Jesus leading me at this stage in my life? Tomorrow I go before the Chapter 13 Bankruptcy trustee. What am I to do now? What will happen concerning the buildings I occupy? What will happen concerning a multitude of matters? I imagine the disciples were thinking like I am too: Jesus had told them at the Last Supper to go back to Galilee. I cannot recall Jesus telling me anything yet. Perhaps He will go before me and show me the way. I think He will. Tomorrow I will be looking to follow Jesus where He wants me to go.

The Grace We Seek: to trust in God's friendship and companionship.

Prayer is a matter of relationship. Intimacy is the basic issue, not answers to problems or resolutions 'to be better'. Many of life's problems and challenges have no answers; we can only live with and through them. Problems and challenges, however, can be faced and lived through with more peace and resilience if people know that they are not alone...and have experienced God's intimate presence.

William Barry, SJ, Letting God Come Close

Week Twenty-Eight

Rejoice always, pray without ceasing, give thanks in all circumstances, for this is the will of God in Christ Jesus for you. Do not quench the Spirit.

1 Thessalonians 5:16–19

Where is the risen Saviour we are learning to know more clearly, love more dearly, and follow more nearly, leading us now? In the words of Micah, to where is He going before us? In the words of Mary Magdalene, go to Galilee and He will meet us there. Where is our personal Galilee? Jesus is always with us. If we are seeking His presence, He is in us already ruling in the Spiritual Kingdom that his death established.

This is my last prayer of imagination for this book:

I think when one dies, it will be good to have at least one person who really loves you. I imagine Mary Magdalene loved Jesus the most, perhaps even more than Jesus' Mother Mary, or even more than the Apostle John. Maybe one cannot love more than a Mother loves, perhaps it was a different kind of love for each of these people. Mary Magdalene is said to be a sinner, but we are all sinners and need to be aware of that reality. Some say Mary Magdalene was a prostitute, but there is no evidence to support that that I know of. There are other ways to sin. Mary was rich – she gave lots of money to support Jesus. She loved Jesus. Jesus was broke. He had enjoyed some times in His life when He had the money He needed to live and occasionally to share with His friends and family when some wealthy people around Capernaum would hire Him to do woodworking for them.

Mary Magdalene hired Jesus one time to make a chest of drawers for her clothes. She had some nice clothes. Some people said she should have worn more of them sometimes, but she wanted to look nice and compelling as she went about town. She was about thirty years old, a beautiful woman with long red hair. The chest Jesus built had hand-cut dovetail drawer joints. He cut the dovetails with a saw, a chisel, a wooden mallet, and a scoring marker. The drawers opened smoothly on wood runners and one would put a little bee's wax on the wooden runners occasionally to make them slide easily. The air would properly whoosh out as one closed the drawers. 'This is just right', thought Jesus. Jesus always remembered making that chest for Mary. She paid Him well and gave Him a hug when He delivered it to her home. Jesus loved Mary too.

After Jesus died, Mary cried all night. It was the Sabbath and she knew she should be sleeping and resting, but she couldn't. All she had ever believed in had been taken away. Mary did not know what to do. It was cool that Sunday morning and Mary got up very early, having tossed and turned all night and she slid out one of the drawers in the chest Jesus built for her as she gently wept under the subdued light of the blood moon that year. There aren't many years the moon looks like that. The Jewish sages had talked about blood moons before, and Mary wondered if maybe God had caused the moon look that way this the year Jesus died. She put on heavier clothing, but not her best because she would be out in a garden area close to the tomb.

Mary went to the tomb and it was empty; Jesus was not there, but angels were. I read it again and I cried as Mary realised it was really Jesus alive again when she found Him in the garden. She loved Him so much and hugged Him again, a long time, just like when Jesus built her chest of drawers. Jesus had to tell her to let loose. It was getting too emotional for both of them, and Jesus had not yet gone to his Father.

Everybody knows this classic resurrection story. I am just filling in some details of how it could have been, letting my imagination which is a gift from God, help me to connect the events as Mary ran along the Judean hills to go tell Peter everything. Mary was the very first Evangelist. A woman was not supposed to be a witness back then, but she did it anyway because Jesus instructed her to go and tell others.

The Grace We Seek
the courage to let God in

I far prefer a Church that has had a few accidents to a Church that has fallen sick from being closed. Go out, go out! Think of what the book of Revelation says as well. It says something beautiful: that Jesus stands at the door and knocks, knocks to be let into our heart.
Pope Francis, The Church of Mercy

Week Twenty-Nine

Two are better than one, because they have a good reward for their toil. For if they fall, one will lift up the other; but woe to one who is alone and falls and does not have another to help.

Ecclesiastes 4:9–10

The personal epiphanies I experience on occasion during my daily Examen are not the final answers to my great questions about life and meaning. I had hoped to have discerned my way forward by now, but I still do not know exactly what to do. It was suggested that I find a spiritual director to accompany me on this path. I am not sure where and how to find one in an effort to continue my quest. I am continually disappointed in my vanity, pride, and conceit. I have offered them up to God and believe they are forgiven.

The Grace We Seek: gratitude for all the gifts in our lives.

As labourers in the vineyard, we make a difference in this world. We do not work alone. We are co-workers with God. We are here to tend the garden and bear fruit that will last. One who works in a vineyard is an optimist; a labourer committed to the long haul, to patient, respectful cooperation with fellow labourers and with the Lord of the harvest.

Peter Schineller, SJ, The Pilgrim Journey of Ignatius

Week Thirty

My sheep hear my voice. I know them, and they follow me. I give them eternal life, and they will never perish. No one will snatch them out of my hand.

John 10:27–28

The point of my prayer this morning was to remember all God has done for me, and to offer it and my entire will back to Him. I have been praying as such in my prayer of formation every day. I think of the phrase in the 'Lord's Prayer'. "Your will be done on Earth as it is in Heaven." I am on Earth. May God's will be done in me! Many things have occurred during this retreat and over the past few years to prepare me for this. I may have lost some physical vitality, but I have gained much more spiritual vitality.

The Grace We Seek: awareness of God's presence and movement in our lives

Whether we are aware of it or not, at every moment of our existence we are encountering God, Father, Son, and Holy Spirit, who is trying to catch our attention, trying to draw us into a reciprocal conscious relationship.

William Barry, SJ, Finding God in All Things

Week Thirty-One

One who spares words is knowledgeable;
one who is cool in spirit has understanding.
Even fools who keep silent are considered wise.
Proverbs 17:27–28

Everything belongs to God. Everything derives its existence from God and everything is already owned by God, so when we pray the Suscipe, then we are only giving back to God what rightly belongs to Him already, and all life in the universe is life that exists in the love and grace of God. The Suscipe prayer is as follows:

"Take Lord, receive all my liberty, my memory, any understanding, and my entire will, all that I have and possess. You have given all to me. To You, O Lord, I return it. All is yours, dispose of it wholly according to your will. Give me only Your love and Your grace, for these are enough for me."

I was thinking of my proclivity to always want to jump out and 'do' something. Maybe it is time to wait, not to just jump out and act. Maybe it is time to just rest a while in God's graceful, loving, and sufficient provision.

The Grace We Seek: the serenity to rest in God's care.

We all need a place inside ourselves where there is no noise, where the voice of the Spirit of God can speak to us, softly, and gently, and direct our discernment. We need the ability to become ourselves—silence, emptiness, an open space that the Word of God can fill, and the Spirit of God can set on fire for the good of others and of the Church.

Adolfo Nicolas, SJ, Superior General's Summary 2012

Week Thirty-Two

Do not be conformed to this world, but be transformed by the renewing of your minds, so that you may discern what is the will of God—what is good and acceptable and perfect.

Romans 12:2

The call of the Spirit is to those outside of the gates of the heavenly city, the Kingdom of God, where all sinners reside, where the Spirit still calls and we get a glimpse of the eternally loving, good God who longs that all would be saved, even those who have rejected His calling in this lifetime. Therefore, I perceive that our St. Ignatian retreat is not really over. It has just begun, and that the Spirit will always call us to know God more clearly, and to follow Him more nearly, to love Him more dearly as we live on into Eternity.

The Grace We Seek: gratitude for the challenges in our lives and the gifts and opportunities that happen as a result.

Above all, trust in the slow work of God. We are, quite naturally, impatient in everything to reach the end without delay. We should like to skip the intermediate stages. We are impatient of being on the way to something unknown, something new. And yet it is the law of all progress that it is made by passing through some stage of instability—and that it may take a very long time.

Pierre Teilhard de Chardin, SJ, Hymn of the Universe

Epilogue

Well, what happens next? In the section of the Exercises called 'The Call of Christ, the King', I felt led to write about the Spiritual Exercises and to promote them. You are reading the book now, born of the journal I kept while making the Exercises. You can visit my website www.SimpleWayCoffin.com to download the original 387–page manuscript. There is no charge for this more detailed journal. One can order a print of the original art used for the cover of this book on the web site.

Since the Exercises, I have passed along my business to someone younger and I am a Spiritual Director and received a Certificate in Spiritual Direction (CSD) through Spring Hill College, a Jesuit college, in Mobile, AL in the summer of 2019. I am in the process of discernment to find where all this will lead. Perhaps you also will want to share what you have learned reading this book and listening to the Spirit, with others. Let God in! May the Spirit lead and bless you!

Suggested Readings

1) *A Year of Prayer, Co-Labouring with the Living Lord, Ignatian Companions on Mission,* by Fr. Tim Brown, S.J., may be a compilation of authors, October 2005 – May 2006, two volumes, one, a Resource Book of 166 pages, the other volume, a Guide Book of 229 pages, spiral bound, cost varies according to availability, may be self-published by Maryland Province Society of Jesus. No ISBN listed. *A Year of Prayer, Co-Labouring with the Living*

2) *Retreat in the real world: finding intimacy with God wherever you are: a self-guided Ignatian experience,* by Andy Alexander, Maureen McCann Waldron, and Larry Gillick, published by Loyola Press, A Jesuit Ministry, 1999, 2009, 308 Pages, Paperback, $14.95, ISBN-13:978-0-8294-2913-8; ISBN-10-08294-2913-1

3) *The Ignatian adventure: Experiencing the Spiritual exercises of St. Ignatius in daily life,* Kevin F. O'Brien, SJ, Published by Loyola Press, A Jesuit Ministry, 2011, 290 Pages, Paperback, $14.95, ISBN-13: 978-0-8294-3577-1; ISBN-10: 0-8294-3577-8.

4) *A-Do-It-At-Home-Retreat, Spiritual Exercises of St. Ignatius of Loyola,* by Andre' Ravier, S.J., Original title in French original: *En Retraite chez soi,* translated by Conelius Michael Buckley, S.J., Published by Ignatius Press, 1991, 233 pages,

Paperback, Price not listed on book, ISBN 0-89870-363-8

5) *Thirty Days on retreat with the exercises of St. Ignatius,* by Paul Mariani, Published by Penguin Group, 2002, 285 Pages, Paperback, Price, $16, ISBN 0-670-89455-9 (hc.); ISBN 0 14 21.9615 0 (pbk.)

6) *The Spiritual Exercises of St. Ignatius, A New Translation Based on Studies in the Language of the Autograph,* by Ludovico J. Puhl, S.J., Published by Loyola Press, A Jesuit Ministry, 1951, 216 pages, Paperback, $5.95, ISBN-13: 978-0-8294-0065-6; ISBN-10: 0-8294-0065-6

7) *Saint Ignatius of Loyola, Personal Writings, Translated with introduction and notes,* by Jospeh A. Munitiz and Philip Endean, Published by Penguin Books, 1996, 413 pages, Paperback, $13.95, ISBN 0 14 04.3385 6

8) *Reimagining the Ignatian Examen*, Fresh Ways to Pray from Your Day, by Mark E. Thibodeaux, SJ, Published by Loyola Press, A Jesuit Ministry, Chicago, 2015, 89 pages, Paperback, $9.95, ISBN-13: 978-0-8294-4244-1; ISBN-10: 0-8294-4244-8

9) *Companions of Christ, Ignatian Spirituality for Everyday Living*, by Margaret Silf, Published by William B. Eerdmans Publishing Company, Grand Rapids, Michigan, Cambridge, U.K., 2004, 115 pages, ISBN 0-8028-2942-2

10) *The Examen Prayer, Ignatian Wisdom for Our Lives Today,* by Timothy M. Gallagher, O.M.V., The Crossroad Publishing Company, 2006, 190

pages, Paperback, $17.95, ISBN-13: 978-0-8245-2367-1; ISBN-10: 0-8245-2367-9

11) *Weeds Among the Wheat, Discernment: Where Prayer & Action Meet,* by Thomas H. Green, S.J., Ave Maria Press, Notre Dame, Indiana, 1984, 204 pages, Paperback, $10.95, ISBN 0-87793-318-9

12) *The First Spiritual Exercises, A Manual for Those Who Give the Exercises,* by Michael Hansen, S.J., Ave Maria Press, Notre Dame, Indiana, 2013, 178 pages, Paperback, $19.95, ISBN-10 1-59471-380-4

13) *The First Spiritual Exercises, Four Guided Retreats,* by Michael Hansen, S.J., Ave Maria Press, Notre Dame, Indiana, 2013, 369 pages, Paperback, $19.95, ISBN-10 1-59471-378-2

14) *Making Choices in Christ, The Foundations of Ignatian Spirituality,* by Joseph A. Tetlow, SJ, Loyola Press, A Jesuit Ministry, Chicago, Illinois, 2008, 124 pages, Paperback, $12.95, ISBN-13: 978-0-8294-2716-5; ISBN-10 0-8294-2716-3

15) *Always Discerning, An Ignatian Spirituality for the New Millennium,* by Joseph A. Tetlow, SJ, Loyola Press, A Jesuit Ministry, Chicago, Illinois, 2016, 247 pages, paperback, $14.95, ISBN-13: 978-0-8294-4456-8; ISBN-10: 0-8294-4456-4

16) *The Friend of the Bridegroom,* by Thomas H. Green, S.J., Ave Maria Pres, Inc., Notre Dame, IN, 2000, 128 pages, paperback, $12.95, ISBN 0-87793-938-1

17) *Finding God in all Things, A Companion to the Spiritual Exercises of St. Ignatius,* by William A.

Barry, S.J., Ave Maria Press, Inc., Notre Dame, IN, 1991, 140 pages, paperback, $13.95, ISBN 0-87793-460-6

18) *Door Through Darkness: John of the Cross and mysticism of everyday life,* by Sister Eileen Lyddon, New City Press, 1995, 175 pages, Paperback, ISBN 1-56548-037-6 (pbk)

19) *The Art of Spiritual Guidance: a contemporary approach to growing in the spirit,* by Carolyn Gratton, The Crossroad Publishing Company, 1992, ISBN 0-8245-1223-5 (pbk)

20) *The Call to Discernment in Troubled Times: New Perspectives on the Transformative Wisdom of Ignatius of Loyola,* by Dean Brackley, The Crossroad Publishing Company, 2004 ISBN: 0-8245-2268-0 (pbk).

21) *Candlelight: illuminating spiritual direction,* by Susan S. Phillips, Morehouse Publishing, 2008, ISBN: 978-0-8I92-2297-8 (pbk).

22) *The Cloud of Unknowing: With the Book of Privy Counsel,* Translated by Carmen Acevedo Butcher, Shambhala, 2009, 276 pages, ISBN 978-1-59030-622-2 (pbk).

23) *Awakening the Creative Spirit: Bringing the Arts to Spiritual Direction,* by Christine Valters Painter and Betsey Beckman, Morehouse Publishing, 2010, ISBN 978-0-8192-2371-5 (pbk).

24) *Close to the Heart: A Practical Approach to Personal Prayer,* by Margaret Silf, Loyola Press, 1999, ISBN 0-8294-1452-5 (pbk).

25) *Looking Into the Well: Supervison of Spiritual Directors,* by Maureen Conroy, 1995, Loyola Press, ISBN 0-8294-0827-4 (pbk).

26) *Addiction and Grace: Love and Spirituality in the Healing of Addictions,* by Gerald G. May, 1998, ISBN 978-0-06-112243-9 (pbk).

27) *Breathing Under Water: Spirituality and the Twelve Steps,* by Richard Rohr, Franciscan Media, 2011, ISBN 978-1-61636-157-0 (pbk).

28) *The Art of Christian Listening,* by Thomas N. Hart, Paulist Press, 1980, ISBN 0-8091-2345-2 (pbk).

29) *A Pilgrim's Journey: The Autobiography of Ignatius of Loyola,* Introduction, Translation, and Commentary by Joseph N. Tylenda, S.J., Ignatius Press, 2001, ISBN 978-89870-810-3 (pbk).

30) *Silent Compassion: Finding God in Contemplation,* by Richard Rohr, Franciscan Media, 2014, ISBN 978-1-61636-757-2 (pbk).

31) *Spiritual Consolation: An Ignatian Guide for the Discerning of Spirits,* by Timothy M. Gallagher, O.M.V., Crossroads Publishing, 2007, ISBN-13: 978-0-8245-2429-6 (pbk).

32) *Inner Compass: An Invitation to Ignatian Spirituality,* by Margaret Silf, Loyola Press, 1999, ISBN-13 978-0-8294-1366-8 (pbk).

33) *Holy Listening: The Art of Spiritual Direction,* by Margaret Guenther, Rowman & Littlefield Publishers, Inc., 1992, ISBN-13 978-1-56101-056-1 (pbk).

34) *Letting God Come Close: An Approach to the Ignatian Spiritual Exercises,* by William A. Barry, S.J., Loyola Press, 2001, ISBN 0-8294-1684-6, (pbk).

35) *Prayer*, by Joyce Rupp, Orbis Books, 2007, ISBN 978-1-57075-712-9

36) *Moving in the Spirit: Becoming Contemplative in Action*, by Richard J. Hauser, S.J., Paulist Press, 1986, ISBN 0-8091-2790-3 (pbk).

37) *Spiritual Direction: Beyond the Beginnings*, by Janet K. Ruffing, R.S.M., Paulist Press, 2000, ISBN 0-8091-3958-8 Pbk).

38) *Care of Mind/Care of Spirit: A Psychiatrist Explores Spiritual Direction*, by Greald G. May, Harper Collins, 1992, ISBN 0-06-065567-4 (pbk).

39) *The Need and Blessing of Prayer*, Karl Rahner; translated by Bruce W. Gillette, by The Order of St. Benedict, 1997, ISBN 0-8146-2453-7, (pbk).

40) *Choosing Christ in the World*, by Joseph A. Tetlow, S.J., The Institute of Jesuit Resources, 1999, ISBN 1-880810-36-0, (pbk).

41) *Finding Christ in the World: a Twelve Week Ignatian Retreat in Everyday Life*, by Joseph A. Tetlow, S.J., The Institute of Jesuit Resources, 2017, ISBN 978-1-880810-82-4, (pbk).

Index